Little Golden Books
Little Golden Books
Little Golden Books
Little Golden Books

What do children learn from a Richard Scarry book?

To be curious about the world around them,
to stay positive and optimistic,
to look for funny surprises,
to take responsibility,
to have good manners and show kindness for others,
and to feel safe and loved in their communities.

—Huck Scarry, son of Richard Scarry

Golden Books
An imprint of Random House Children's Books
A division of Penguin Random House LLC
1745 Broadway, New York, NY 10019
penguinrandomhouse.com
rhcbooks.com
richardscarry.com

Library of Congress Control Number: 2025948933
ISBN 979-8-217-12531-9 (trade) — ISBN 979-8-217-23583-4 (ebook)

Manufactured in China
10 9 8 7 6 5 4 3 2 1

The authorized representative in the EU for product safety and compliance is Penguin Random House Ireland, Morrison Chambers, 32 Nassau Street, Dublin D02 YH68, Ireland, https://eu-contact.penguin.ie.

EVERYTHING I NEED TO KNOW I LEARNED FROM a Richard Scarry Golden Book®

A GOLDEN BOOK • NEW YORK

BAKERY
WATCHES
TOYS
1
2
A
MILK
HOT DOGS

It's a busy world.

Greet the morning
with joy!

Best Word Book Ever, copyright © 1963.

Always make your bed—
that's your first success of the day!

Grab a brush.
Tame that bedhead.

Enjoy a good hearty breakfast!

Dress to impress!

TRUCKS
GRO
50
5 4 3

Get to know your neighbors.

Be helpful!

Set a course for discovery.

The Bunny Book, written by Patricia Scarry, copyright © 1955.

There are interesting jobs
everywhere you go!

Sometimes things
don't go as planned.

Measure twice and cut once.

What Do People Do All Day?, copyright © 1968.

Don't be too hard on yourself.

Keep fit!

Have you tried yoga?

Get regular checkups
by the doctor,

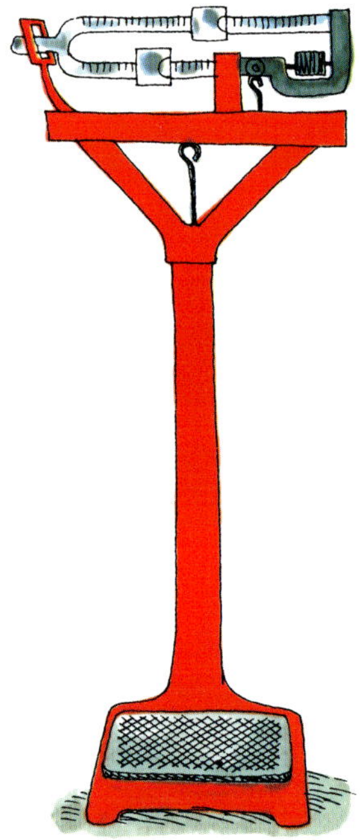

and visit the dentist at
least twice a year.

Dance like no one
is watching, even
when they are.

It's okay to feel shy
sometimes,

but it’s so much better to be outgoing!

An unexpected card
can brighten someone's day.

Don't forget to play!
It is fun and keeps you healthy.

Chipmunk's ABC, written by Roberta Miller, copyright © 1963.

Always be careful
when crossing the street.
Don't forget to look both ways!

Polite Elephant, copyright © 1963.

Lend a helping hand—or trunk—
whenever you can.

Discover your own style.

What Do People Do All Day?, copyright © 1968.

Find a hobby that makes you happy!

Appreciate beauty,

and fill your life with art!

The Bunny Book, written by Patricia Scarry, copyright © 1955.

Read!

Share your talents.

Teamwork makes the dream work!

Say hello to someone who's feeling down.

Please don't be rude!

Follow the rules.

Don't let chores frighten you!

Lend a helping hand . . . or foot!

Save your money.

Give hugs freely.

GRADE
A

Share the fun!

Don't be afraid
to try new things!

The Country Mouse and the City Mouse, written by Patricia Scarry, copyright © 1961.

Go outside.

Plant a garden!

Make delicious discoveries in the kitchen.

To make something wonderful,
you have to break a few eggs.

Take small bites!

Drive politely!

Recycle.

Mend!

Repair it!

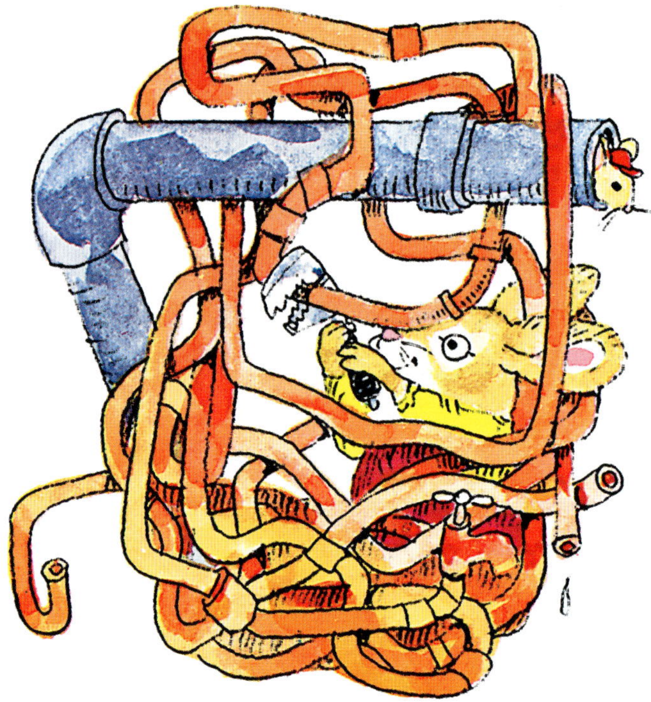

Stay focused . . .

When life
gets too busy,

Cars and Trucks and Things That Go, copyright © 1974.

slow down.

LIQUID DETERGENT
MUSTARD
CHINAWARE THIS SIDE UP
AMBULANCE
POLICE

Don't panic!

Never give up!

Busy, Busy Town, copyright © 1994.

Indulge!

Best Picture Dictionary Ever, copyright © 1966.

Follow your bliss.

Embrace the unexpected.

March to the beat of
your own drum!

Travel!

Busy, Busy World, copyright © 1965.

The world is full of fantastic sights

and interesting people.

Travel in style!

Cars and Trucks and Things That Go, copyright © 1974.

FRESH
EGGS

Take time to enjoy,

Cars and Trucks and Things That Go, copyright © 1974.

but watch where
you're going!

Take only pictures,

Best Picture Dictionary Ever, copyright © 1966.

and leave only footprints
(but not indoors).

There's no bad weather—
only wrong clothing.

Best Christmas Book Ever!, copyright © 1981.
Great Big Schoolhouse, copyright © 1969.

Accept help when you need it!

Sometimes you have to take
the sour with the sweet.

If life gives you pickles . . .
have a pickle party!

Busy, Busy World, copyright © 1965.

Treat yourself,

but don't overdo it!

When you feel you're sinking,

remember, you can do big things!

Best Counting Book Ever, copyright © 1975.

Step back to see
the big picture,

What Do People Do All Day?, copyright © 1968.

but appreciate the little things.

EAT AT JOE'S
CHIEF

There's a town of people ready to get busy helping you!

Embrace sleep!

Good night!

Good Night, Little Bear, written by Patricia Scarry, copyright © 1961.

Little Golden Books
Little Golden Books
Little Golden Books
Little Golden Books
Little Golden Books
Little Golden Books